# FROM METAL
# To Music

## A Photo Essay
## by Wendy Davis

# Children's Press

A Division of Grolier Publishing
New York  London  Hong Kong  Sydney
Danbury, Connecticut

**Created and Developed by The Learning Source**

**Designed by Josh Simons**

**Acknowledgement**: We would like to thank the many people and organizations who provided technical assistance with this project. Their help is greatly appreciated.

**Photo Credits:** Copper Development Association: 8-17, front and back cover; Frank Stewart for Sony Classical: 5; Jean Moss for the Yamaha Corporation of America: cover (inset); Lisa Berg for the Mannes College of Music: 6; Mannes College of Music: 1; Robert Egan: 3-4, 30-31; The Selmer Company, Inc.: 32; United Musical Instruments U.S.A., Inc.: 18-28; Village Flute & Sax Shop, NYC: 29; Yamaha Corporation of America: 7.

**Note:** The actual brass instrument-making process often varies from manufacturer to manufacturer. The facts and details included in this book are representative of one of the most common ways of producing brass instruments today.

**1 2 3 4 5 6 7 8 9 10 R 06 05 04 03 02 01 00 99 98 97**

Library of Congress Cataloging-in-Publication Data
Davis, Wendy
    From Metal to Music  :  a photo essay / by Wendy Davis.
        p.    cm. — (Changes)
    Summary: Describing the steps in making trumpets, tubas,
and other horns. From the mining of the copper ore to the shaping
of the finished poduct.
        ISBN  0-516-20707-5    (0-516-26068-5  pbk.)
            1. Bass instruments—Construction—Pictorial works—Juvenile literature.
1. Metal—work—Pictorial works—Juvenile literature.
[1. Brass instruments—Construction.  2. Metalwork.]    I. Title.
II. Series: Changes (New York, N.Y.)
ML933.D381997
788.9' 1923                                                96-4718
                                                              CIP
                                                              AC MN

Pick up a horn. Play some music.
Play it by yourself . . .

4

. . . or with friends.

Play it on a stage . . .

. . . or in a marching band.

You can play a horn just about anywhere.

But where do horns come from?

Copper ore is the first step. Ore is rock that is part metal. The ore is taken from a mine . . .

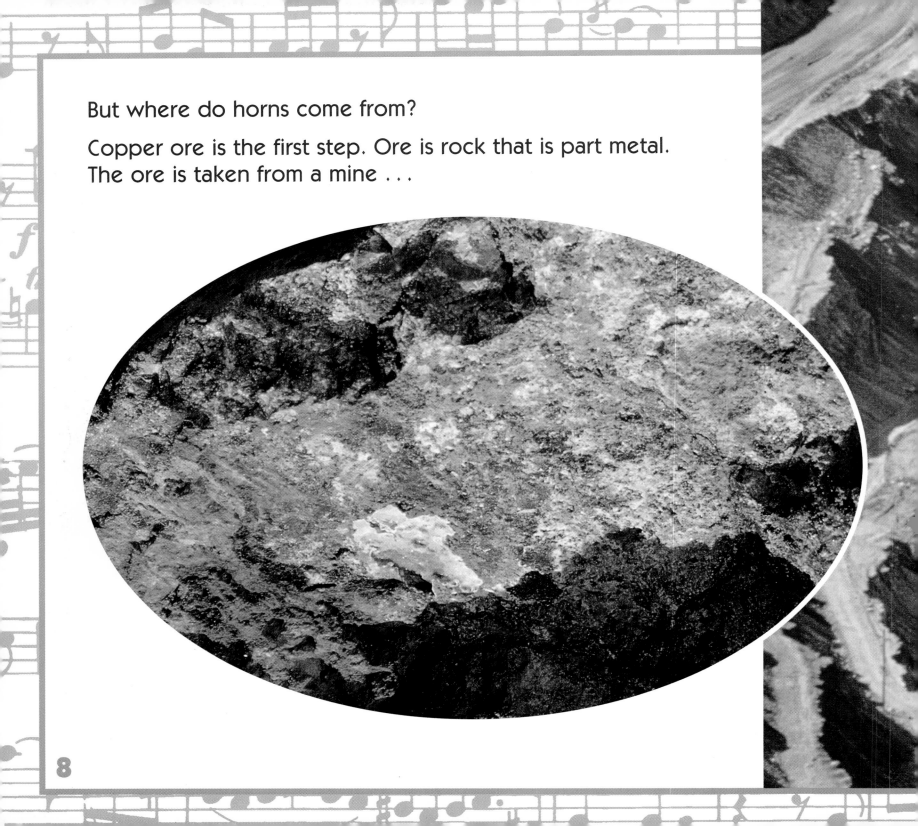

. . . and loaded onto a dump truck.

It is carried to a copper mill and crushed into walnut-sized pieces.

A grinder mashes the ore into powder. At the same time, it separates the copper from the rest of the rock.

A huge furnace turns the copper powder into fiery liquid.

Another metal, called zinc, is added. Together, copper and zinc form brass, which is what horns are made of.

Now the liquid brass is poured into molds . . .

and formed into thick bars,

or thin sheets,

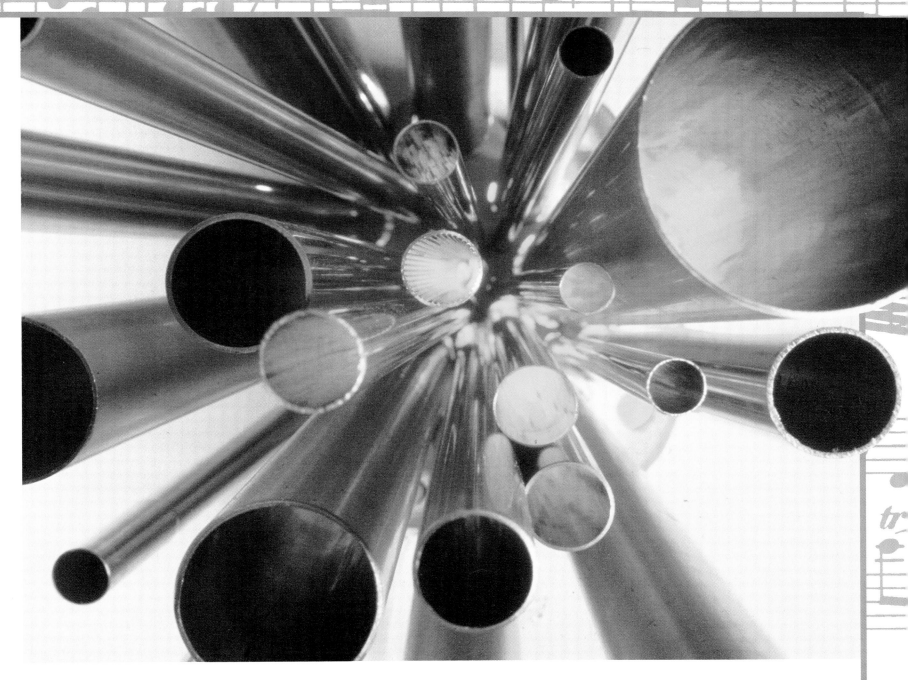

or even long, skinny tubes.

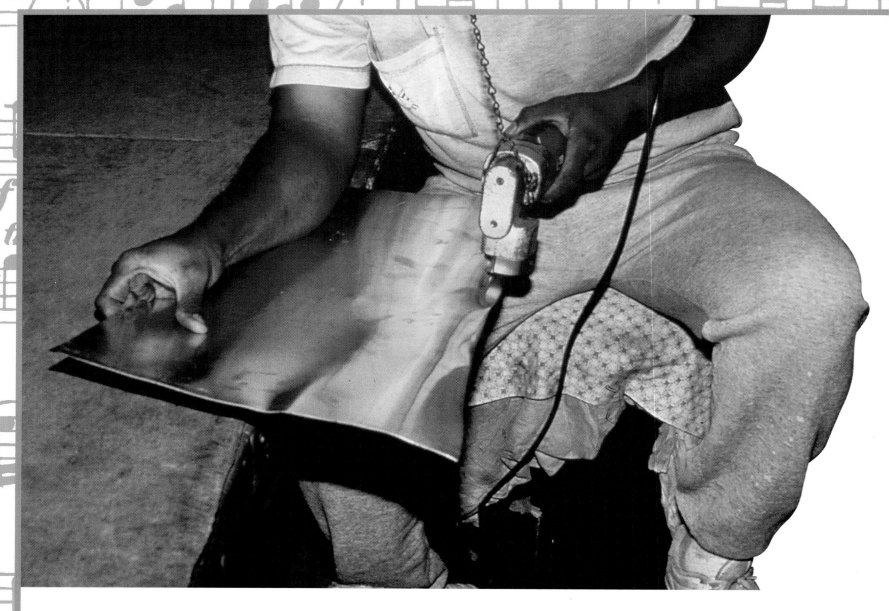

Then the metal goes off to the music factory. Here, sheets of brass are cut . . .

. . . and shaped.

Some pieces are made into bells and attached to tubes.
The bell is the front part of a horn, where the music comes out.

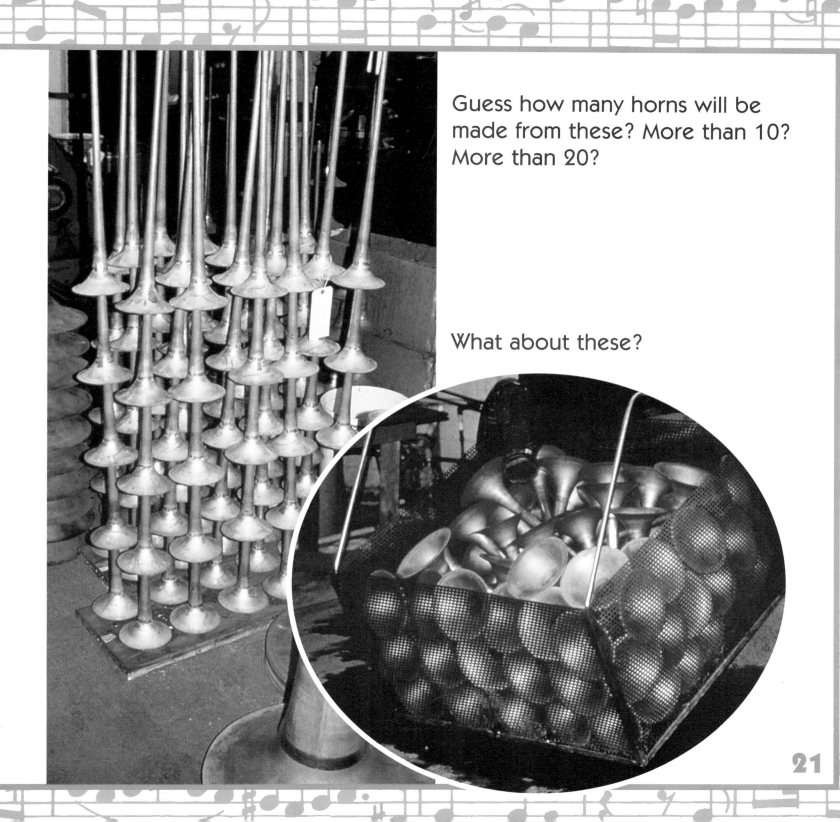

Guess how many horns will be made from these? More than 10? More than 20?

What about these?

21

There are many kinds of horns. Each has certain bends and twists that give it a special sound.

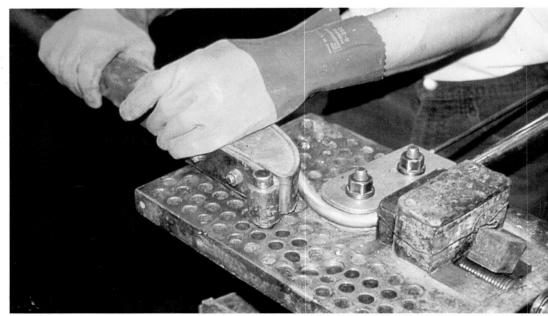

These horns may look ready for playing, but they aren't.

That's because horns need valves or slides to make the different notes in the musical scale.

Valves are attached by heating small bits of metal. This is called soldering (SAH-der-ing).

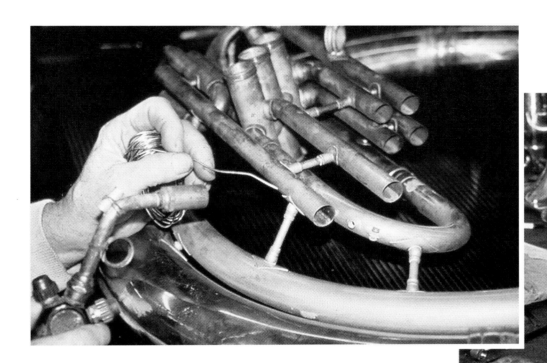

Other parts are fitted together.

Then each horn is
buffed and polished . . .

. . . inside and out.

The horns are tested for tone and action. Is the sound clear and bright? Do the keys and valves move easily?

Finally, the horns are polished one last time.

Now the metal has
become a horn.
But is it music?

Not yet. It's still missing
one more thing —

You!

# MORE ABOUT HORNS

**Tuba**
Tubas are the biggest brass instruments in the orchestra. There are many kinds of tubas, each with its own special sound.

**Saxophone**
A saxophone is made of brass. You blow onto a saxophone's reed to make music on it.

**Trumpet**
A trumpet has only three valves. But with them you can play every note in the musical scale.

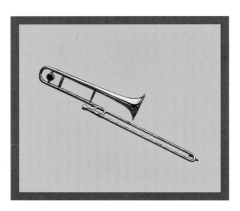

**Trombone**
There are no valves on most trombones. You make notes by moving the long metal slide back and forth.

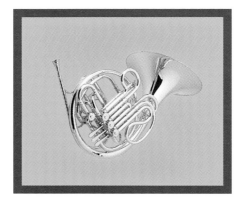

**French Horn**
The French Horn looks like a small instrument. But if you unroll all the tubing, it is more than 12 feet long!

**Sousaphone**
Sousaphones are so large that you can walk with one wrapped around your body. That is why they are so popular in marching bands.

**What other instruments can you name that are made from metal?**